CULTURAL CRIMES: THE LAW IT IS AND THE LAW OUGHT TO BE

VOLUME 2, ISSUE 1 OF BRILLOPEDIA

SHIVANSH PATHAK AND YASHANA MALHOTRA

ISBN 979-888606999-0

Contents

Preface

"Start writing, no matter what. The water does not flow until the faucet is turned on".

-Louis L'Amour

Hundreds of students and professors are contributing their work to Brillopedia, we are here to provide ample information about Law and Contemporary issues. Our aim is to provide a platform for today's generation to express their views and ideas on law and contemporary law.

Publication

This research paper is published in volume 2, issue 1 of Brillopedia

Authors

Shivansh Pathak

Yashana Malhotra

INTRODUCTION

'Culture' and 'Crime' are those two words which bring in a plethora of paradoxical perceptions when used simultaneously. The basic understanding of both the concepts is inevitable as to the study of Cultural Crime and its jurisprudence. The most pertaining note to this study is that there has been no deliberate interest or effort put in to attribute a real meaning or a definite understanding to the term of Cultural Crime in its generic term. Even the subject matters of cultural criminology transcending traditional notions of crime and crime causation to include images of illicit behavior and symbolic displays of law enforcement; popular culture constructions of crime and criminal action; and the shared emotions that animate criminal events, perceptions of criminal threat, and public efforts at crime control, hesitates to endeavor in this process of defining cultural crime. Instead we are provided with examples like hate crimes, sexual offences, honour killings etc in order to make a perception of our own on the issue of cultural crimes of socio-biological, criminological and jurisprudential importance. When the legal academics itself is uncaring about the phenomenon of cultural crime, the study of Law pertaining to cultural crimes, the law it is and the law it ought to be, should start from the basic understanding of 'crime', 'culture' and 'cultural crime'.

CHAPTER TWO

THE ACTIVITY CALLED 'CRIME'

A crime is a sin consisting in the committing by deed or word of that which the law forbiddeth, or the omission of what it hath commanded. So that every crime is a sin; but not every sin a crime.[1]

Crimes are 'mala in se,' or bad in themselves, and these include all offences against the moral law; or they are 'mala prohibita,'bad because prohibited, as being against sound policy which, unless prohibited, would be innocent or indifferent.[2]

Crime is a social phenomenon since because it envisages both how individuals conceive crime and how populations perceive it, based on societal norms.[3].

A normative definition views crime as deviant behavior that violates prevailing norms – cultural standards prescribing how humans ought to behave normally. This approach considers the complex realities surrounding the concept of crime and seeks to understand how changing social, political, psychological, and economic conditions may affect changing definitions of crime and the form of the legal, law-enforcement, and penal responses made by society.[4]

Natural-law theory therefore distinguishes between "criminality" (which derives from human nature) and "illegality" (which originates with the interests of those in power). Lawyers sometimes express the two concepts with the phrases *malum in se*[5] and *malumprohibitum*[6]respectively. They regard a "crime *malum in se*" as inherently criminal; whereas a "crime *malumprohibitum*" (the argument goes) counts as criminal only because the law has decreed it so.[7]

[1] See Michael L. Morgan, Classics of Moral and Political Theory (4th edn2005) p.649

[2] **Mala**prohibita ("wrongs that are prohibited") criminal offenses proscribe conduct that is wrongful simply because a legislature has chosen to criminalize it; examples of such **crimes** include speeding and disposing of hazardous waste without the appropriate permit. In contrast, **mala** in **se** ("wrongs in themselves") **crimes** are those that traditionally have been regarded as inherently evil; examples include rape and larceny.

[3] The label of "crime" and the accompanying social stigma normally confine their scope to those activities seen as injurious to the general population or to the State, including some that cause serious loss or damage to individualsQuinney, Richard, "Structural Characteristics, Population Areas, and Crime Rates in the United States," *The Journal of Criminal Law, Criminology and Police Science*, 57(1), p. 45-52

This view point has a close relation with natural law theory, where the existence of immoral law is only a temporal fiction. The theory of natural law posits that the nature of the world or of human beings underlies the standards of morality or constructs them[4]. Since society considers so many rights as natural (hence the term "right") rather than man-made, what constitutes a crime also counts as natural, in contrast to laws (seen as man-made).

[5] **Malum in se:** "A wrong in itself; an act or case involving illegality from the very nature of the transaction, upon principles of natural, moral, and public law... An act is said to be **malum in se when it is inherently** and essentially evil, that is, immoral in its nature and injurious in its consequences, without any regard to the fact of its being noticed or punished by the law of the state." Black's Law Dictionary 959 (6th ed. 1990).

[6] **Malum**prohibitum: "A wrong prohibited; a thing which is wrong because prohibited; an act which is not **inherently** immoral, but becomes so because its commission is expressly forbidden by positive law; an act involving an illegality resulting from positive law." *Ibid.* at 960.

[7] Adam Smith illustrates this view, saying that a smuggler would be an excellent citizen, "...had not the laws of his country made that a crime which nature never meant to be so." See, The Distinction Between Mala Prohibita and Mala in Se in **Criminal** Law, 30 Colum. L. Rev. 74 (1930).

CHAPTER THREE

THE WORD 'CULTURE'

The word *culture* comes from the Latin root *colere* (to inhabit, to cultivate, or to honor). In general (as according to Sociology, Social Science, Anthropology and ethnology), it refers to human activity; different definitions of *culture* reflect different theories for understanding, or criteria for valuing, human activity. But our preference of definition for understanding the term 'cultural crime' has nothing to do with the word '*culture*[1]' referring to elite goods and activities such as *haute cuisine*, high fashion or *haute couture*, museum-caliber art and classical music etc.

Sir Edward B. Tylor wrote in 1871 that "culture or civilization, taken in its wide ethnographic sense, is that complex whole which includes knowledge, belief, art, morals, law, custom, and any other capabilities and habits acquired by man as a member of society"[2]

Culture is traditionally the oldest human character, its significant traces separating *Homo* from australopithecines, and Man from the Animals, though new discoveries are blurring these edges in our day.

[1] Matthew Arnold (1822-1888)had consistently explained "... culture being a pursuit of our total perfection by means of getting to know, on all the matters which most concern us, the best which has been thought and said in the world. See Arnold, 1882, *http://www.library.utoronto.ca/utel/ nonfiction_u/arnoldm_ca/ca_all.html*

[2] See E. **Tylor,** Primitive **Culture** 1-69 (2d ed. 1873; Reprinted In 1958) discussing the development of **culture** and the theory that **culture** evolves with the move from savagery to civilized life.Evolutionary social scientists developed **Tylor's** theory of cultural "survivals" in their work. His theory later became a prominent mechanism by which jurisprudents and legal historians such as Holmes explained the persistence of outdated legal rules. Herbert Hovenkamp, "Evolutionary Models in Jurisprudence" 64 Tex. L. Rev. 645 (1985)

CHAPTER FOUR

CULTURE AND CRIME

Though there are basic explanations for what crime is and what culture is; the most of the sociologists, criminologists and academic research scholars have shown an unresponsive attitude towards the explanation required for what significance it will perpetualize when both the words come together one after the other. This had indubitably resulted in the lack of a 'definite' definition for the term 'Cultural Crime'. And the primary concern of this article being *jurisprudence of cultural crimes*, it had become inevitable to deduce a definition for cultural crime.

Primarily, the adjective 'Cultural' denotes distinctive of the ways of living, derived from the totality of the inherited and shared ideas, beliefs, values, and knowledge of a society[1]; ie which are built up by a group of people; "influenced by ethnic ties"[2]

Thus according to normative definition, if both the words co exists one after the other it would be a paranoid, because crime is a deviation from the normal behavior of the society and cultural denotes the distinct ways of living naturally found in the society. Then what does the term 'Cultural Crime' exactly denotes? What does the crime here refers to, "mala in se' crime or 'mala pohibata' crime?

This paradox has its answers or reasons for its existence in the evolution theories of anthropology and sociobiology. Attentive to the theory of evolution, they assumed that all human beings are equally evolved, and that the fact that all humans have cultures must in some way be a result of human evolution. They believed biological evolution would produce a most inclusive notion of culture, a concept that anthropologists could apply universally to all non-literate and literate societies, or to nomadic and to sedentary societies.[3]

But through the course of their evolution, human beings evolved a significant universal human capacity to classify experiences, and encode and communicate them symbolically. Since these symbolic systems were learned and taught, they began to develop independently of biological evolution.[4]

Sociobiologists supports these aspects of culture through the understanding of the concept of the *meme*[5]. The idea is that there are units of culture, *memes*, roughly analogous to *genes* in evolutionary biology.

[1]The American Heritage® Dictionary of the English Language, Fourth Edition copyright ©2000 by Houghton Mifflin Company.Updated in 2009.Published by Houghton Mifflin Company. See Also <u>Collins English Dictionary – Complete and Unabridged</u> © HarperCollins Publishers 1991, 1994, 1998, 2000, 2003

[2].See Thomas C. Holt, The Problem of Race in the 21st Century 12-13 (2000).

[3]In criminal law, the doctrine of evolution by natural selection quickly turned into a debate over individual responsibility and the causes of crime. Social Darwinists believed that genetics determined criminal behavior, and that nothing reformed the "criminal type"; instead, the criminal should be placed where he could not harm society. Reform Darwinists, however, believed that the state could manipulate the environment so as to contain the propensity toward criminal behavior or perhaps even restructure society so as to virtually eliminate criminal behavior.

[4]in other words, one human being can learn a belief, value, or way of doing something from another, even if they are not biologically related. Thus people living apart from one another develop unique cultures, but elements of different cultures can easily spread from one group of people to another. At this juncture of studies and research took the view that culture is not only a product of biological evolution, but as a supplement to it, it is also the product of human adaptation to the world. anthropologistsClifford Geertz (1973: 33 ff.) has argued that human physiology and neurology developed in conjunction with the first cultural activities, and Middleton (1990: 17 n.27) concluded that human "'instincts' were culturally formed", since culture is dynamic and can be taught and learned, making it a potentially rapid form of adaptation to change in physical conditions. Some anthropologists have argued that heterogeneous societies are nevertheless bound by some unifying cultural system, and that heterogenous elements are better understood as subcultures. Others have argued that there is no unifying or coordinating cultural system, and that heterogeneous elements must be understood together to form a multicultural society . In addition

to the aforementioned processes, by 19th century, the world has been characterized by migration on a major scale due to colonial expansion and forced migration through slavery, and due to the globalization effects of 20th century, many societies developed into an existence, culturally heterogeneous.

[5] introduced by Richard Dawkins in his 1976 book *The Selfish Gene*

CHAPTER FIVE

DEFINING THE TERM 'CULTURAL CRIME'

This acculturation has resulted in the lining up the word crime to the adjective cultural. This means in a ethnically heterogonous world or society some distinct ways of living may have local sanction within a specified subculture or social group-lets, but such acts on the other hand may fall in 'mala in se' or 'mala prohibita' categories when relatively overlooked by the society in general.[1] Laws vary within the same culture from time to time as well as across different cultures.[2]

However the modern-day criminologists, the superset cultural crimes have now made inclusive of sex crimes, pornography and domestic violence against women and minors, and even some times, economic exploitation and crimes against environment.[3]

Thus based on the victims and their ethnic groups cultural crimes can be classified into two:

1. Crimes within the cultural group or group-let. (mainly gender and age discrimination; lookism and weightism are other reasons). eg:- Bali – 'killings for sacrifice', honour killings, dowry system, corporeal punishment like whipping and spanking and nailing.
2. Crimes trans-cultural (racial, linguistic, ethnic, caste, and religious discrimination). eg;- hate crimes

But both the classes of cultural crimes, the offender targets a victim, by the reason of his prejudicial treatment of his membership perceived in a certain social group, usually defined by racial group, religion, sexual orientation, disability, class, ethnicity, nationality, age, gender, gender identity, or political affiliation.

Thus accordingly as a definition, the term 'cultural crime' would refer those crimes which are generally motivated or which are the resultant sins of prejudicial, biased and xenophobic attitudes existing among the individuals or ethnic fragments in a heterogeneous cultural society.[4]

[1] See, The Distinction Between Mala Prohibita and Mala in Se in **Criminal** Law, 30 Colum. L. Rev. 74 (1930).

[2] See generally, Ellis, L., & Walsh, A. *Criminology: A global perspective* (2000). Until the Harrison Narcotics Act of 1914, there were few legal restrictions in the United States on the sale, possession, or use of most drugs such as heroin and cocaine. Following the Harrison Act, many drugs became controlled substances, their possession became a crime, and a brand new class of criminals was created overnight. Stalking is hardly novel behavior, but certain high-profile cases moved the state of California to recognize the dangers inherent in the practice and to pass the nation's first antistalking law in 1990.Until the U.S. Supreme Court invalidated sodomy statutes in *Lawrence v. Texas* sodomy was legally punishable in many states. Most states targeted only homosexual sodomy, but a few extended the reach to include heterosexual sodomy, even between consenting spouses. *Lawrence v. Texas* 539 US 558 (2003

[3] But do the reasons for these transgressions of liberty and fraternity belong to the phenomenon of acculturation? To a greater extent, we have to nod yes. Yet still evils like dowry system do not belong to cross-cultural evils, instead exists within a same cultural system or sub-cultural. Even though this is true here we see an intolerant attitude towards between two classes or sects belonging to same cultural super set. In the case 'dowry', it exists in Indian cultural system between social classes defined by sex.

[4] Emphasis supplied.

CHAPTER SIX

THE LAW, ENFORCEMENT AND PENAL SANCTIONS – AN APPRASIAL IN THE CONTEXT OF CULTURAL CRIMES

No express provisions defining cultural crimes or its sanctions.

First and foremost, it is highlighted that no prudent and express law provisions explain cultural crime in its generic term or the various forms of it. Though there are laws against discrimination and express provisions regarding dowry prohibition in India, there are no much appreciated legislations on the issues of cultural crimes such as hate crimes, honour killings and corporeal divine punishments etc. The charges on such crimes are made under the penal code provisions of abetment, murder, and assault respectively

The present day legal provisions calls only for individual responsibility and punitive justice.

But they can hardly account for the inherent sensuality, ambiguity, and irrationality of crime itself. The accounts for various contemporary confluences of crime and culture are much beyond from the circumspection of these provisions.

The aggressive policing of alternative subcultures and their styles; the mediated consumption of crime as commodified titillation and entertainment; and the shifting and always contested boundaries between art and pornography, music and political provocation, entertainment and aggression, crime and resistance, are some of the forefront example of cases which the legal system lacks understanding. The ambiguities pertaining to the liability and criminalization of these activities are still a let-known head ache of the policy makers.

Recognition of 'cultural defense' in the criminal justice system

On the other hand, most of the antidiscrimination statutes by definition are concerned with group-based differences, yet there is no presumed unlawfulness is identified because the Constitution itself contains an antidiscrimination command, statutes that merely mirror this mandate and reflect a concern with group-based differences cannot be suspect.[1]

Every antidiscrimination statute aimed at racial discrimination, and every enforcement measure taken under such a statute, reflect a concern with race. That does not make such enactments or actions...automatically "suspect' under the Equal Protection Clause."[2]

Such policies and principles of law provides the recognition of **Cultural defense in the criminal justice system.** These advocates of this school of politics and legal research claim that recognition of a cultural defense will advance two desirable ends consistent with the broader goals of liberal society and the criminal law: (1) the achievement of individualized justice for the defendant; and (2) a commitment to cultural pluralism[3].

Many courts have nevertheless permitted the introduction of cultural evidence in criminal trials. In recent years, defendants have successfully raised cultural defenses in cases with fact patterns as disparate as rape[4], child molestation[5], politically motivated suicide[6], and violence connected with spousal infidelity[7]. Ostensibly, such cases, to the extent that they reflect judicial receptiveness to the notion that foreign culture may mitigate a foreign defendant's culpability, represent victories for the twin rationales of cultural pluralism and individualized justice.

No needful legal research.

The absence of definition of the term cultural crime, itself implicates the aversion and unwariness of the legal system towards the issue. But why does this happens? The answer is that the dominant modes of research and criminological analysis are quantitative data analysis and survey research methodology, the major approaches are objectivism and reductionism. And the emphasis laid down is that all these are based on the assumptions of instrumental rationality[8]. Since the emergence of academic disciplines structured on 'rational' lines, there has been a seemingly irrevocable disjuncture between scientific knowledge and everyday experience, with the former dominating research into the latter[9].

This is a methodology where lived experience becomes 'pathologised' or 'marginalised' by the official accounts of crime. The result is a nurtured ignorance of the reality of 'real' life, 'lived' life, 'everyday' life. The lack of compassion in calculative research approaches, made such methods unable to either grasp or understand crime or the causes of crime[10]. This further leaves cultural significance of crime unaccounted and unincorporated into the jurisprudential learning.[11]

[1] Raso v. Lago, 135 F.3d 11, 16 (1st Cir. 1998)

[2] Ibid.

[3] The Cultural Defense in the Criminal Law, <u>99 Harv. L. Rev. 1293, 1296 (1986)</u>; Michael Fischer, Note, The Human Rights Implications of a "Cultural Defense," 6 S. Cal. Interdisc. L.J. 663, 679-85 (1998)

[4] Deirdre Evans-Pritchard & Alison DundesRenteln, The Interpretation and Distortion of Culture: A Hmong "Marriage by Capture" Case in Fresno, California, 4 S. Cal. Interdisc. L.J. 1 (1994) (discussing People v. Moua, No. 315972-0 (Cal. Super. Ct. Feb. 17, 1985) (unpublished decision)

[5] Farah Sultana Brelvi, "News of the Weird": Specious Normativity and the Problem of the Cultural Defense, 28 Colum. Hum. Rts. L. Rev. 657, 658 (1997).

[6] Richard Lacayo, Whose Peers?, Time, Sept. 22, 1993, at 60

[7] People v. Wu, 286 Cal. Rptr. 868 (Ct. App. 1991)

[8] CULTURAL CRIMINOLOGY, Jeff Ferrell, *Blackwell Encyclopedia of Sociology.*

[9] 'Anti-social behaviour:: inertia, resistance and silence.' Jean Baudrillard (1990:10)

[10] Scott Lasch remarks: In a society that has reduced reason to mere calculation, reason can impose no limits on the pursuit of pleasure- on the immediate gratification of every desire no matter how perverse, insane, criminal or merely immoral. For the standards that would condemn crime or cruelty derive from religion, compassion, or the kind of reason that rejects purely instrumental applications and none of these outmoded forms of thought or feeling has any logical place in a society based on commodity production (1979: 69)

[11] Similarly, changes in the collection and/or calculation of data on crime and adjustments to such crime statistics, allied with the experience of people in their everyday lives, leaves the structural realities fluid and often contentious, thereby causing no clear consensus sanction on a given

norm or on the cultural crime. And in turn in those cases where no clear consensus exists the drafting of criminal law by the group in power to prohibit the behaviour of another group may seem to some observers an improper limitation of the second group's freedom, and the ordinary members of society or of that of the subculture will have less respect for the law or laws in general.

CHAPTER SEVEN

THE REASON FUNDAMENTAL FOR THIS MISLEADING NOTION – POLITICALLY MOTIVATED STATISTICS AND RESEARCH METHODOLOGIES

Multiculturalism has coincided with a resurgence of identity politics, which involves demands for recognition of a social subgroup's cultural uniqueness.

This quantitative rational scientific approach is epitomized by those government agencies that their role being the production of 'suitable' facts to support governments and their existing and future political agendas[1].

It is the role of administrative criminology to help in this process[2]. Many potential issues are thus kept out of politics and research through the operation of social forces or through individuals' decisions[3].

Multiculturalists insist that cultural pluralism has made this nation/ society strong and that immigrant groups or subcultures must not be compelled to sacrifice their unique heritages. Thus, dominion society should learn from and help to celebrate the unique customs, history, and languages of its immigrant/ sub cultural groups[4].This had become the motto of political authorities of every state so as to not to loose their power.

[1]Presdee: 2004

[2] For a recent example of this practice at work within British criminological research see Tombs and Whyte (2003).

[3] The political promises of progress, equality, and liberty are woven into the seams of history alongside the threads of failure. So the power does want to prevent issues actually reaching the agenda or the decisional arena and hence becoming matters of open dispute. , See 'Third Dimension of Power'; Lukes' (1974: 24)

[4] James J. Orlow, America's Incoherent Immigration Policy: Some Problems and Solutions, 36 U. Miami L. Rev. 931, 937 n.4 (1982)

CHAPTER EIGHT

THE VISION OF THE LAW OUGHT TO BE – PRINCIPLE AND METHODOLGY

The legal system confronting or comprehending cultural crimes has to go two fundamental changes:

1. Basic transformation of the principle of law or the policies from their lenient disintegrated view of administrative criminology to a stringent standardized view of crimes in the context of the globalised world.
2. Structural remodulation of research methodology by incorporating cultural criminology and socio-biological preferences of manhood.

Multiculturalism should have to take a back seat to the interests of victims and potential victims of criminal acts perpetrated by "cultural defendants.

On this account, the cultural defense, while ostensibly advancing individualized justice for the defendant from a foreign culture, trammels the rights of immigrant women and children who are often the victims of **"cultural" crimes.** Not only should that of women and children, interests of victims include the right to obtain protection and relief through a nondiscriminatory application of the criminal law[1].

The dominion society's interests in maintaining order and forging bonds among people by imposing a common set of cultural values should militate against recognition of the cultural defense[2]. And from then, an assassin who kills a political leader because he believes it is right to do so cannot ask that he be judged by the standard of a reasonable extremist[3].

The abolition of the disparate application of the criminal laws is one of the primary concerns of the rule of law. The commentators have subsequently observed that the Equal Protection and Due Process Clauses embody an "antidiscrimination principle" guaranteeing that similar individuals should be accorded with similar treatment by the government[4]. Thus criminal-defense doctrine must recognize the group-based differences in order to prevent discrimination is not equivalent of a state action that grants preferences to members of a minority group based on race or national origin.[5] And henceforth the selective denial of the government's protection to disfavored minorities will have to be rendered unconstitutional.[6]

Cultural defendants in respect to the highly relevance to natural justice should receive fair recognition at the hands of the criminal justice system. But on the other hand Courts must take account of these crucial differences between foreign defendants and the dominant group in order to provide the former with the same basic protection "in respect to life and liberty" available to all other persons[7].

The Compassionate and non-biased research methodology

At the outset we need to understand how Cultural crime comes into being, the causes of the crime and the creation of the criminal whilst appreciating more that crime can only be created through social relations made within a dominant culture and determined by a dominant morality.

For know what essentially motivates crime, and superior descriptions and explanations on crime we must over throw the system of quantitative rational scientific approach towards criminology, crimes and criminalisation which only generates numerical life and adopt a compassionate, cultural and socio-biographical accounting on crimes.[8]

The quantitative rational scientific agenda has intrinsic problems in the difference between rationality and irrationality, because the rational social world is always politically biased, but on the other hand the real world of everyday life has purity in its functioning. Thus Quantitative research must in the end 'add up' and show clearly and conclusively what is going on and what is to be done. Or else excrescence of facts descending from social science will bury the real nature and causes of crimes committed culturally in everyday life[9].

This is where we need to understand that people, subjects- are not simply the 'blind' result of economic relations. In negotiating social structures they both interpret their lives and invest meaning in their lives.

Yet there are no unlimited options for them, there are only so many possibilities open to them, including crime and transgression. In this way they act both individually yet within a collective, a class. Here is the anarchic carnival of everyday life where 'joy and the fulfillment of desires prevail over morality'. After all the 'fun' of gambling is more powerful than work with its promise of 'release' from poverty and failure[10].

The law should not forget that all sections and segments of society have emotions: they hurt, they hate, they envy, they love, they feel anxious; their stories of transgression are full of the emotions of everyday lives lived within the structures of loss, envy, and the sheer celebration of their place in society.

The legal system then compassionately shall realize that the everyday life is essentially about lived loss...of what we thought we could have, could posses, could be, could experience. When the 'loss' is more in focus, people are more 'shamed' than ever before, shamed by failure, by social position, by poverty, by being bad parents, by bad behaviour and this shame produces violence, destruction and social despair. Loss hurts- compensation culture results. Here is where people find the culture of binge drinking, of criminalized fun and enjoyment, a culture that has become defined (in the broadest of terms) as anti-social behaviour. The policy makers then have to see crime as a story of unfulfilled lives and desires.[11]

The law should then take account of people clinging hopelessly to the idea of a classless meritocracy. The identities reflecting either freedom or oppression had created the idea of crime and sin, and if we seek through culture to soften the chaffing of the chains of dominance and natural honour[12], and definitely the Cultural Crime rate shall numerically fall down.

[1]DorianeLambelet Coleman, Individualizing Justice Through Multiculturalism: The Liberals' Dilemma, 96 Colum. L. Rev. 1093, 1097 (1996).at 1127

[2] John C. Lyman, Note, Cultural Defense: Viable Doctrine or Wishful Thinking?, 9 Crim. Just. J. 87, 105-11 (1986); Julia P. Sams, Note, The Availability of the "Cultural Defense" as an Excuse for Criminal Behavior, 16 Ga. J. Int'l & Comp. L. 335, 339-40 (1986).

[3] Model Penal Code and Commentaries 210.3

[4] Paul Brest, Supreme Court 1975 Term - Foreword: In Defense of the Antidiscrimination Principle, 90 Harv. L. Rev. 1 (1976)

[5] Peter Rubin observes that the antidiscrimination cause has been dealt a serious blow by the tendency of both common citizens and jurists to "conflate antidiscrimination laws... with affirmative action provisions whose constitutionality can be determined... only after they have been subjected to searching judicial scrutiny." Rubin, supra note 143, at 565

[6] DeShaney v. Winnebago County Dep't of Soc. Servs., 489 U.S. 189, 197 n.3 (1989). The legal system ought to be should consider that the charge that laws designed to protect members of various groups actually grant these groups special treatment has become increasingly common, [See Rubin, supra note 143, at 570] the Supreme Court explicitly repudiated the "special rights" critique in Romer v. Evans.[517 U.S. 620 (1996).] Striking down Colorado's infamous initiative banning laws protecting homosexuals from discrimination, the Court held: "The amendment withdraws from homosexuals, but no others, specific legal protection from injuries caused by discrimination....We cannot accept the view that Amendment 2's prohibition on specific legal protections does no more than deprive homosexuals of special rights." [Id. at 631.]

[7] Farber & Sherry, supra note 129, at 309 (quoting Representative John Bingham's statement on the principle underlying the Equal Protection Clause)

[8] *Theoretical Criminology* (Volume 8, Number 3, 2004). Mike Presdee , The Story Of Crime: Biography And The Excavation Of Transgression

[9] As Baudrillard remarked, in typical style:

the rational systems of morality, value, science, reason, command only the linear evolution of societies, their visible history. But the deeper energy that pushes even these things forward comes from elsewhere. From prestige, challenge, from all the seductive or antagonistic impulses, including suicidal ones, which have nothing to do with a social morality or a morality of history of progress (1990: 72-3)

[10] Lefebvre, 1971: 16

[11] (Steedman. 1986:111), Melanie Klein (1975: 306-7)

[12] Horder describes "natural honour" as the good opinion of others founded in the assumption that the person honoured by the good opinion was morally worthy of such esteem and respect. It was distinguished from acquired honour by the fact that, whereas acquired honour had positively to be earned, natural honour was established negatively: it was simply one's due if one had not failed in any principle virtue (principally courage)., Jeremy Horder, Provocation and Responsibility 25-30 (1992).